Manufacturing Engagement

98 Proven Strategies to Attract and Retain Your Industry's Top Talent

Manufacturing Engagement

98 Proven Strategies to Attract and Retain Your Industry's Top Talent

By Lisa Ryan

Published by Grategy Press, Cleveland, Ohio

Grategy, LLC

3222 Perl Ct.

North Royalton, OH 44133

216-359-1134

lisa@grategy.com

www.grategy.com

www.LisaRyanSpeaks.com

Manufacturing Engagement

98 Proven Strategies to Attract and Retain Your Industry's Top Talent

Lisa Ryan

Grategy, LLC

Other Books by Lisa Ryan

The Upside of Down Times:

Discovering the Power of Gratitude

From Afraid to Speak to Paid to Speak:

How Overcoming Public Speaking Anxiety Boosts Your
Confidence and Career

The Verbal Hug:

101 Awesome Ways to Express Appreciation

Express Gratitude, Experience Good

A Daily Gratitude Journal

Thank You Notes:

Your 30-Days of Gratitude Workbook

52 Weeks of Gratitude

Transformation Through Appreciation

52 More Week of Gratitude

Thank Your Way to Happiness

Thank you, Dale Evraets, for being the best boss ever!

You celebrate with me in the good times and keep my spirits up through tough periods.

You are the epitome of the kind of manager every person should be blessed with in their career.

Thank you for your guidance, support, and friendship over the past twenty years. I appreciate you!

When you tell someone you appreciate them,

You create a memory.

When you write it down,

You create a treasure.

~ Lisa Ryan

Table of Contents

PART 1

Build a Foundation of TRUST

"When the trust account is high, communication is easy, instant, and effective." -Stephen R. Covey

Have an "open-mind" versus an "open door" policy.

A true "open door" policy is difficult to maintain. With lean production scheduling and tight deadlines, you don't always have time for employees to pop in and ask you a question. After all, if they know they can always come to you to solve their problems, what incentive do they have to figure it out on their own?

An "open mind" policy shows that you are open to frank discussion and you will set appropriate boundaries that work for you and your team. Let your employees know that you are there for them when they truly need you, but not for every single complaint or question.

Action Ideas:

1. Make sure that no matter what you hear, you don't "kill the messenger." Listen without interruption and ask for your employee's suggestion in solving the issue.

2. Have a "thanks for sharing" attitude instead of a "yeah but" attitude. If you fight or argue about the points that your team member is trying to make, they will stop sharing.

3. Never ask a question that you don't really want the answer to. Become a master of the "Poker Face" and provide a safe haven for them to share thoughts and ideas with you.

Learn from and benchmark top performers.

When you notice your "rock star" employees accomplishing great things, take the time to learn what they are doing differently from everyone else. Incorporate their ideas and methods into new hire training. Utilize these best practices to benchmark what other departments and different shifts are doing. Always look for ways to improve your processes.

If one employee figures out a tactic that works, don't let his/her efforts go to waste. If that person is doing something well, then there's a good chance that those same ideas can be used for others in your facility.

Questions to ask:

1. What motivates you about your job?
2. What challenges you?
3. How/what do you delegate to others?
4. How do you communicate with your team?
5. What shortcuts have you discovered?
6. What resources do you still need?
7. How can we help?

What do you want to learn from your top talent?

Be enthusiastic about the future.

Unless you are confident in your plant's ability to succeed, how do you expect your employees to believe they have a stable future?

Be a cheerleader - no, not the kind with pom-poms. Encourage and support your team. Cheer them on. Broadcast the good things that are happening. Create a culture where employees want to share their positive experiences, instead of just complaining about the bad times. When you incorporate good news in your communications, you improve staff commitment, engagement, and understanding.

Bonus: It's easier to create content for your newsletter, blog, or marketing articles as you learn all the new and exciting stories you have to tell.

Action Ideas:

1. Keep an eye out for situations where your employees are making a difference and share it with the rest of your team.

2. Use good news as a learning opportunity. Share what happened and then cite the takeaways that can inspire others to model the good behavior.

3. Make sure to help people look good when they participate. Provide multiple ways colleagues can respond and add to the good news, comment on the success of others, and share their own experiences in similar situations.

Flatten your organizational structure.

A flat company structure empowers your employees to take charge of their jobs, make better decisions and feel a greater level of responsibility for the company's success. By getting rid of some of the layers of management, you facilitate more communication as well. Asking your staff for their input leads to more support for the decisions made, and you'll see fewer power struggles behind the scenes.

Don't make employees jump through a lot of hoops to share their ideas. The only thing red tape halts is progress. When you give your staff access to leadership, it helps them feel like they are heard and can make a difference.

As the number of Millennial and Gen Z employees increase, you will see a shift away from the autocratic way of running a business. Employees want to contribute, and your best ideas may come from the least expected sources.

How can you give your employees greater access to leadership?

_____

_____

_____

_____

_____

Be open and honest in sharing information.

A company went through a restructuring. Instead of keeping employees in the loop, they announced the move through two conference calls. During the first call, twelve people found out their jobs were "eliminated, effective immediately." During the second call, the HR Manager read the names of their colleagues caught up in the downsizing to the remaining staff.

Because everyone was caught unaware, it took the staff a long time to rebuild any sense of trust with leadership. Employees met every conference call with suspicion. They attended every meeting with a sense of fear.

If the organization had been up front and let their employees know that some changes may be coming, they could have minimized the long-term damage.

Action ideas:

1. Employees may not always like what you must tell them. Be upfront and tell them anyway.

2. When you restructure your organization for financial reasons, ask your employees for ideas on how to make a smoother transition. You may be surprised with their creativity and insight.

3. Make sure any employees you release due to cutbacks are thanked for their service and taken care of financially as much as you can.

Offer competitive wages and benefits.

Although managers often feel that throwing money at an employee is the number one way to keep that person engaged, it is not. However, if your wage scale is not up to industry standards, people will look elsewhere.

When everything else is equal, people take the higher paying job.

It is worth paying for quality talent. When you do so, you can save your company significant money in the long run in these three areas:

Healthcare. When your employees are satisfied, they are more likely to be healthy, thus decreasing the healthcare premiums you are paying.

Recruitment and training. If your employees are pleased with their benefits, they are less likely to leave. You won't have to train new staff continually.

Productivity. Gallup research shows that workers who are "highly satisfied" with their jobs are up to 50% more productive at work.

What do you need to review regarding your employees' wages and benefits?

_____

_____

_____

Encourage management to mingle with the staff.

An HR manager shared that her managers are required to learn the names of all the people that report to them. If supervisors are unwilling to make an effort to do this, she fires them. At first blush, that sounds a little extreme, doesn't it? However, how would you feel working for a boss that didn't even know your first name – really?

Walk around the shop and greet people by name. Look for reasons to have a short conversation when possible. Challenge yourself to find shared interests with your staff. Yes, it's true, some of your employees are more willing to share their personal lives than others. Whichever way they respond is fine – it's making the effort that counts.

Action Ideas:

1. Regularly schedule time with each of your employees. Often, a simple five-minute check-in will suffice.

2. Use icebreakers and other social activities that allow team members to learn interesting facts about each other and get to connect on a personal level.

3. If you're "not good" with remembering names, take steps to change that. Dale Carnegie Training and other companies offer excellent guidance on recalling names.

Create strong relationships with your employees.

Your employees want you to see them as more than a name on their uniform shirt. Keep it simple. Find out what they like. Cat people? Dog people? Favorite sports teams? Hobbies? Learn what they value, and they will value you.

One icebreaker you can use is "Two Truths and a Lie." Here's how it works: Break into groups of up to eight people. Have everyone write down three statements, two of which are true, and one is a lie. Each person takes a turn reading their comments. The others in the group try to guess which one is the lie. The reader does not fess up until everyone has guessed. Keep track of how many people each person fools.

While working with a restaurant chain, we discovered that two of their kitchen managers had cooked for two different Presidents of the United States. Even the company owners did not know this. How cool is that?

Action Ideas:

1. Use short icebreakers to add interest to your meetings.

2. Organize activities that allow employees to spend time together as a group outside of work.

3. Recognize your employees' achievements as they happen. Don't wait to acknowledge good work.

Get rid of toxic employees.

If you have a toxic employee in your shop, correct the situation or let that person go. A hostile "lone wolf" can do more damage than their productivity (or lack thereof) is worth.

Of course, from a legal standpoint, documentation is critical. Record exactly what the employee did and the negative impact he/she had on the team. This action not only protects you from wrongful termination lawsuits, but it also shows that you made every effort to help the employee, but he chose not to do so.

Just one problem employee can destroy the culture of an organization. And, when a problem employee causes others to leave, who jumps ship? Your worst employees or your best ones? Take the steps you need to create order and harmony amongst the staff.

1. Have a correction action plan in place. Offering coaching and retraining before the formal discipline process shows the effort you put forth to help your employee change.

2. Train your managers in proper documentation techniques. If it is not written down, it didn't happen.

3. There are no employees that you can't live without. It's never easy to fire someone, but sometimes that is your only option. It's a business decision. The rest of your team will breathe a sign of welcome relief.

Allow open and honest feedback.

Some employees may be uncomfortable speaking their minds. There may be numerous reasons for this, but it's critical for you to create the space for them to do so. Promote and practice respectful candor. When employees don't feel they have a voice, they may hold back valuable information, ideas, and solutions that could propel your company forward. Don't be the "Emperor who is not wearing clothes" in your shop.

Notice that the optimal word here is "respectful." Play nice. Allowing honest communication goes not give people the license to be rude, crude, or mean-spirited.

If asking staff for feedback is new for you, start small. Acknowledge the responses you receive and encourage more detailed replies to your inquiries.

Action Ideas:

1. Focus on the future. Ask what you can do better going forward instead of focusing on what you did poorly in the past.

2. Be specific in what you want. Instead of the overly broad, "What do you think?" ask about particular parts of the project that you are discussing.

3. Let them vent without interruption. Sometimes people need to let off steam and don't need you to "fix" anything. As long as venting doesn't become a habit, be okay with an occasional outburst.

Consistently conduct exit interviews.

It's often difficult when an employee decides to move on. Don't take anyone's leaving for granted. Every manager and every hourly employee have a reason for leaving. Find out what it is in an exit interview. Treat any information received as valuable data that will help you make better decisions going forward.

Some of the topics you'll want to cover in your exit interview include: overall job satisfaction/ dissatisfaction; specific reason for leaving; frustrations experienced on the job; the corporate culture; relationships with supervisors and team members; adequacy of compensation and benefits; and anything else you would like to capture for future posterity.

The point of doing exit interviews is to use the information acquired. Some of it will be difficult to hear. There will be other things that you have no control over. Do what you can to make small changes and over time, you will see big changes.

Key points to discover in your exit interviews:

_____

_____

_____

_____

_____

Treat your staff better than you treat your customers.

Remember, your employees are your internal CUSTOMERS. How you take care of them is a good indication as to how they will treat your clients.

I worked for a manufacturer that put their priorities in this order – Employees, Customers, Leadership. That is exactly correct. Take care of your staff and treat them fairly. Exceed their expectations. When you set high standards for workers and empower them to do the right thing, they will treat your customers with the same regard.

As tough as it is to hear, leadership is third on the list. The better you make your employees look, the better they will make you look. Also, remember to share the credit and accept the blame. Nothing is worse than a manager who throws their employees under the bus. If your employees are not doing their job well, the problem may be you.

Action Ideas:

1. Want to know what would make your employees happy? Ask them.

2. Make sure you maintain your employee gathering areas as well you take care of management and client areas.

3. Let your team know how much you appreciate their contributions to the company.

Share successes up the organization.

Make sure that upper-level management is aware of significant employee contributions. When hourly workers receive an acknowledgment from leadership, they feel valued, simply by realizing that their boss is paying attention to who they are and what they do.

The recognition needs to be timely to be meaningful. When Renee won a national sales contest, it took her manager three weeks to personally congratulate her. By then, it was way too late. A short while later, she left the company.

According to a Harris Poll of 1000 workers, 63% of employees feel that they do not receive recognition for their achievements. Forty-seven percent say their managers take credit for their ideas and 36% say their managers don't know their names. How do you prevent your workers from joining these statistics? Read on.

Action Ideas:

1. Ensure the amount of recognition matches the effort and the results. Overpraising for average performance makes the attempt less meaningful.

2. Be specific. Let your team member know the details of what they did to deserve such praise.

3. Copy upper management on the congratulatory emails you send to staff. Encourage leaders to send a positive reply to the employees recognized.

Acknowledge tenure in smaller increments.

To keep employees longer, try rewarding shorter terms of tenure. Depending on your turnover rate, why not give recognition for one-year or three-years of service – instead of waiting for a five-year anniversary before you acknowledge them.

Organizations who give service awards generate employee morale. Make a big deal of the event. A service award handed out without some sort of pomp and circumstances does not achieve the same effect as those that are publicly extended.

The acknowledgment doesn't have to be big. A signed card by the leadership team with a personal note may be a nice touch – particularly if it is sent to them at home.

Action Ideas:

1. Write it down. Have all your employees and managers sign an Anniversary card and encourage them to write a personal note in the card. Form letters do not have the same effect.

2. Give a gift. Present your staff member(s) with a special token of your appreciation for his/her years of dedicated service.

3. Let them eat cake. Find out what kind of cake or special treat your employee enjoys most and bring that to. Make sure you personalize the cake with their name and years of service.

Watch your facial expressions.

Smile. Greet your employees with a friendly face. People can not only see a smile; they can "hear" one as well, so remember this while you're on the phone.

Author, Tonya Reiman says, "Smiling demonstrates confidence, openness, warmth, and energy. It also sets off the mirror neurons in your listener instructing them to smile back, she says. Without the smile, an individual is often seen as grim or aloof."

Your employees react to the expression they see on your face. When you are concentrating on what they are saying, with your brows furrowed, they may think you are angry with them. Try to keep your expression as neutral as possible when you are listening to what staff has to say.

Action ideas:

1. Make a point to say, "Hello," using your employee's name. Smile or at least nod when you walk by them. Your staff will see you as more friendly and approachable.

2. Keep a mirror by your phone and make sure you are smiling when you are speaking on the phone. It literally changes your tone of voice.

3. Be aware of the fact that the corners of your mouth tend to turn down at the corners as you age. Focus on keeping a neutral expression.

Give tangible evidence of a job well done.

Express your appreciation verbally and/or write it on a note—even a post-it note will work. The recipient will NOT throw that letter away!

Remember, when you tell someone you appreciate them, you create a memory. When you write it down, you create a treasure.

At a luncheon keynote, I shared the power of post-it notes. One attendee scribbled a plus sign on five sheets of paper and handed one to each person sitting at his table, letting them know how they were a positive influence in his life.

One of the receivers of the note excitedly shared with me how thrilled she was to receive this memento. It meant a lot to her – and it was only a plus sign on a piece of paper. This stuff works!

It doesn't take a lot to make someone's day.

What can you do to encourage your managers to thank their subordinates more consistently?

_____

_____

_____

_____

_____

_____

Give your undivided attention.

Put down the phone, stop texting, look away from the computer. When your employee approaches you with a question, problem or issue, make full eye contact, keep a neutral expression, and fully listen.

Simply by being present, you are giving your employee a gift. Yes, it's true.

However, you don't always have time to give your employees the undivided attention they seek. Let him or her know that you are in the middle of something and schedule a time for you to have the conversation – and stick with it. Make your staff your priority, and you'll create a foundation of trust.

Keep yourself from distractions by muting your phone and turning it over on your desk, so you don't notice the texts, emails, and Facebook notices popping up.

Action Ideas:

1. Sincerely focusing on employees may feel uncomfortable at first. Focus on specific actions and keep trying until it feels natural.

2. If you're having a difficult time relating to an employee, challenge yourself to find one good thing about him or her. You'll change the energy you exude around them and will have a good chance of forming a positive relationship.

3. Remember, this concentrated focus works equally well on friends and family too!

Have your employees' backs.

Foster employee engagement by building a foundation of trust with your team. When your colleagues and workers know that you will stand behind them, they are more likely to make better decisions, try new things, and take calculated risks than if they don't feel that you will support them.

When mistakes occur, discuss what happened with our employee, and what they learned from the error. Then move on.

Your job as a leader is to share the credit during times of celebration and take the blame when things go wrong. When asked during informal polls during training sessions about their "worst manager of all time," the number one answer is the manager who throws them under the bus. Don't be that person!

Action Ideas:

1. Ask your subordinates how you can better support them. Be okay with whatever answer they give you and learn from the feedback.

2. Roll up your sleeves and pitch in to help when a staff member is in a pinch.

3. Be the first to acknowledge and celebrate the good work of your workforce. As Dale Carnegie said, "Be lavish in your praise."

Ask about your employees' level of satisfaction.

Employees are more likely to participate in short, pulse-type surveys than long-winded questionnaires. For any "tech-phobic" staff, make sure you invest in a simple system and provide the necessary training to provide feedback.

Include both open-ended and closed questions to get the full picture of what's going on. The most important thing is to make sure you act on the feedback you receive.

Nothing is worse than providing information in the hopes that something is finally going to change, and then hearing "crickets" instead of seeing action. Survey employees regularly, perhaps once a quarter, but not so much that they get burned out from all the polls.

What are some of the specific things you would like to learn from your employees about their level of engagement?

_____

_____

_____

_____

_____

_____

Respond quickly.

Answer the phone and respond to staff emails within 24 hours of receiving them. By taking a few moments to respond to your employees, you send a powerful signal that they are a priority. Your prompt action emphasizes their importance more than just your words ever could.

Because you have timelines, due dates, and priorities that you need to get done, you do not always have the luxury of stopping what you are doing and addressing the employee's issue immediately. You can, however, explain the situation and schedule a more convenient time to connect with them. Then do it.

Action Ideas:

1. Respond immediately to an email or text to let your employee know you received their message.

2. If you can't take care of their issue right away, schedule a more convenient time to speak with them.

3. For difficult conversations, do NOT respond via email or text. It's difficult to read emotion into a written document, and your employee may misinterpret what you are saying. Pick up the phone or meet them in person to convey difficult news.

PART 2

HELP Your Employees Succeed

Excellence is an art won by training and habituation. We do not act rightly because we have virtue or excellence, but we rather have those because we have acted rightly. We are what we repeatedly do. Excellence, then, is not an act but a habit. ~Aristotle

Train to refresh and enhance knowledge.

New employees automatically go through training. During this orientation period, they learn the company's mission, vision, rules and regulations and the conditions in which they will be working.

Sometimes organizations tend to forget about their existing employees when it comes to refreshing and expanding their knowledge base. Make learning a constant in your company.

Here are just a few of the benefits of ongoing training:

Improves employee morale. Training gives employees the feeling of job security and greater job satisfaction.

Requires less supervision. Well trained workers can get the job done with less time and effort.

Enhances promotability. As employees acquire advanced skills, they become a greater asset to the organization.

Reduces accident risk. Errors often occur because a lack of the knowledge and expertise required to do the job.

Increases productivity. Properly training employees require less time, money and resources to get the job done.

When you train, you will retain!

Invest in your employees.

During a conference presentation, I asked the audience members what they did to help their employees grow within the organization. One woman raised her hand and shared that her company gave each worker $1,500 per year to invest in whatever personal or professional development they wanted.

You could hear the collective gasp, as one woman uttered out loud what everyone else was thinking, "We have 500 employees. We don't have that kind of money laying around." I asked the first woman, "How many of your staff take advantage of this offer?" She said, "About 3-5% of them."

It reminds me of the old HR cartoon when the CFO and the HR manager are talking. The CFO says, "Well, what if we invest all this money in training our employees and they leave?" To which the HR manager replies, "Yes, but what if we don't train them – and they stay?"

Who do you want to stay with your company?

Action Ideas:

1. Survey your employees to see what topics are of most the interest to them.

2. Make sure you present training opportunities as an investment in the employee, and not a punishment.

3. Offer lunch and learning sessions, so everyone is on the discussion.

Teach managers to motivate and inspire

Leadership training programs need to be an ongoing part of your professional development offerings. No matter how long your managers have been with your organization, training needs to play consistent role in their career plan.

By providing opportunities for professional development; you create a trickle-down effect that benefits the entire organization.

Training reinforces the good habits that leaders have and teaching them new skills. Look for programs that help leaders manage their time more effectively, learn to set realistic expectations about themselves and their team members and encourage feedback from their managers, peers, and subordinates.

Look at conducting in-house programs so that all your managers can have the same conversation. Consider sending managers off-site to get a fresh perspective and interact with people from different industries.

Ideas for leadership training:

_____

_____

_____

_____

_____

_____

Promote from within whenever possible.

Give your employees opportunities to learn, grow, and expand their knowledge base, so that those workers who want to can achieve their career goals.

Even though the flattening of most organizations means that the chances to "climb the corporate ladder" are much lower than they used to be, there are lots of ways for you to provide the additional training. Check out online courses and different learning resources your current vendors may offer.

When you ask an employee what they want from their career, and you help them to achieve their professional pursuits, you build a strong foundation of loyal employees who will go the extra mile for you, because they know you are taking care of them.

Action Ideas:

1. Offer training and education opportunities to your employees. Those who take you up on the offer may be your emerging leaders.

2. Make sure you train your new managers. Taking your best machine operation and promoting him/her may create your worst new manager without adequate training.

3. Empower your employees to do their job in the best way they see fit. Don't micromanage. Stay out of the way and make it safe for them to come to you if they have questions.

Develop training materials for specific situations.

Let your employees develop protocols based on real-life situations in the workplace. With a record number of baby boomers leaving the workforce, it's critical that you capture the knowledge and expertise that will soon be walking out the door. By taking advantage of the knowledge you have in-house, while you still have them, you'll be better equipped to create procedures that endure for the future.

Be on the lookout for humorous or ridiculous customer service stories — share what happened, and the employee's successful response to the situation.

If there wasn't a satisfactory conclusion, write down some of the lessons learned so that people know what NOT to do when that same situation occurs again.

How do you do this?

Assess Your Needs: What are the areas that your team needs the most assistance and support? Start there.

Design Your Materials: You may want to find articles you like and look for ways to adapt them to your specific needs.

Conduct Training Sessions: Make sure that all employees know and understand the material. Train groups of people so that they are on the same page.

Assess the Results: What went well? What would you change for next time?

Repeat.

Hold yourself and your managers to high standards.

Lead by example in all you do. Problems arise when managers do not follow the precedent they expect others to adhere to. Reasons for bad behavior may range from a lack of knowledge to overall sloppy practices. Correct whatever needs to be fixed and set the standard for excellence.

When supervisors ignore important quality measures in production or are continually allowing the shop floor to be disorganized, it is detrimental to the company's future. Your actions do speak louder than your words, so as Gandhi says, "Be the change you want to see."

Encourage 360-degree feedback and take heed of what employees share with you. Look for the golden nuggets in the responses you receive. Accept any criticism with "Thank you for sharing" and nothing more. If you argue, they will never give you their honest opinions again.

Action Ideas:

1. Always take responsibility. Share the credit, accept the blame. Don't throw your employees under the bus.

2. Praise early and often. Catch team members "in the act" of doing things well.

3. Roll up your sleeves. Do your part and pitch in. You set the example when you make sure that what needs to get done, gets done.

"I love to be micromanaged," said no employee ever!

Don't be what Peggy Drexler of *Forbes* refers to as a "helicopter boss." When you hover over your employees, you create a barrier to trust. Yes, you want to check in with your staff regularly, but give them space. Show them that you trust them, and be there for them when they need your support.

Successful leaders look to the fact that the job is getting done correctly. They are not necessarily concerned with *how* it gets done. Give your employees the opportunity to do things the way they see fit. After all, if the employee completes the job on time and on budget, does it really matter if it's not done exactly the way you would have done it?

Action Steps:

1. If you tend to be a control freak, look for one "baby step" you can take to release control and let your employees succeed (or fail) on their own.

2. Write down the traits that you admire in your favorite boss of all time. What can you do today to let those traits come out in you?

3. Give your staff opportunities to develop new skills. Note their strengths and let them further develop the skills they already have.

Treat employees fairly.

Remember, fair does not necessarily mean equal.

Treating your employees in a fair manner means that you take the time to get to know them and you understand their specific circumstances. If you have a staff member going through a tough time, it's highly likely that their performance may suffer a bit.

Feelings of unfairness lead to lost productivity, disgruntled workers and a lack of trust, resulting in high turnover and low morale.

If your managers are lacking the skills necessary to appropriately manage, motivate, and discipline their workers, sending them for a day of training may do wonders for them. An off-site seminar where they can learn from other new supervisors may be just what they need to succeed.

How do you ensure you and your leaders are treating your employees fairly?

_____

_____

_____

_____

_____

_____

Use mistakes as opportunities.

Create a safe environment for employees to admit when they've made an error.

There's a story of an engineer back in the beginning days of IBM who made a mistake that cost the company a million dollars. The engineer came into Thomas Watson's office knowing Watson was going to fire him. Instead, Mr. Watson asked him, "Why would I fire you? I just spent one million dollars educating you." He never made that blunder again.

A Plant Manager made a mistake that almost cost the company their biggest buyer. After jumping through a lot of hoops, the manager saved the account, but it was a close call. Now she begins her staff meetings with "Who messed up worse than I did this week, and what did you learn from it?" By being vulnerable with her own slip-up, she creates a safe environment for her staff to let her know the real story – instead of hiding the truth out of fear of reprisal.

Learn from your mistakes – and move on.

Action Ideas:

1. Mistakes happen. If you need to, watch the movie "Frozen" several times and learn to "let it go!"

2. See number one.

Create an onboarding process that rocks!

The chances are good that when your employee accepted your job offer, they were probably interviewing at other places too perhaps even with your competitors. Just because they took your job doesn't mean that the calls with other offers will stop.

In the first two weeks of work, your employees are deciding if they really want to stay. If they get an offer from another company that sounds better than what they have with you, you will lose them. All that time, money and effort you spent in hiring them will go for naught.

Some organizations have gone so far as to create viral videos showing what it's like to work there. Why not have some fun and show your candidates and new hires what a terrific organization they can join if they come on board with your company.

Ideas for better onboarding:

1. Connect with new hires before they start

2. Make their first day memorable

3. Introduce them across department lines

4. Ease them into the paperwork

5. Define expectations early and often

6. Ask for their feedback

7. Give them time to adjust to their new role

8. Communicate your culture to make sure they fit

Make sure that your new employee's first day is not leading up to their last day too quickly.

There's value in learning during lunch.

All work and no learning make for a dull team. Give group leaders permission to hold "Lunch and Learn" sessions.

Set up a training portal that your workers can access for their professional development. Check out the many free and low-cost programs available online and offsite.

Giving your team opportunities to learn on their own helps you to figure out which staff members are self-motivated enough to take advantage of additional training (watch those people!).

When you offer "lunch and learns" for anyone who wants to attend, you'll have a group of individuals in the same room, learning the same things, and having the same conversations. There is strength in numbers and the more the word spreads about how fun these programs are, the more people will take advantage of them over time.

Action Ideas:

1. If your programs have a slow start, don't give up. It takes time to catch on.

2. Ask attendees how you can make the sessions more beneficial - and listen to their ideas.

3. Encourage people to invite their colleagues to attend. Using word of mouth will get the numbers up.

Make it right.

An audience member shared that she was in a meeting where she was berated by the rest of her team for dropping the ball on the part of a project she was responsible for completing.

During a break, her supervisor pulled her aside and let her know that HE did not send her the documentation she needed. He not only apologized, but he took ownership of his mistake in front of the whole group when the meeting went back into session.

Did he diminish his stature with this employee and the rest of the team? NO! He elevated it. He built a level of trust and accountability and led by example as to what to do in this kind of situation.

Action Ideas:

1. Admit your mistake immediately and without excuses. Take responsibility for what you did. The sooner you accept what happened, the sooner you can make it right.

2. Don't blame others. Throwing people under the bus will worsen the situation and cause distrust with your team.

3. Prepare yourself for the consequences. They may not be as bad as you think – on the other hand; they may be worse. Suck it up.

Provide educational resources.

Many of your employees are looking for ways to be better tomorrow than they are today. Training is an essential part of professional development.

Have a resource library and train your employees how to use it. Assign a certain topic or chapter to an employee that they can share at an upcoming meeting or training session. Many of your staff may not have picked up a nonfiction book since high school, so educate them on the value of learning and sharing new ideas and teach them how to do it.

These are the four levels of competence:

Unconscious incompetence: the employee doesn't know what they don't know.

Conscious incompetence: the worker now realizes that they lack knowledge in a subject.

Conscious competence: the employee is learning how to do a job, but they must think about it as they go along.

Unconscious competence: the employee now knows the job so well they don't have to think about it to do it perfectly.

By exposing your workers to new concepts, new ideas and new ways of thinking, you will open them up to all kinds of new possibilities for them to succeed.

Keep up-to-date programming.

Monitor your training program's effectiveness and close any gaps. Ask your staff what training would most benefit them and why.

Don't necessarily stick to topics that are immediately relevant to your employee's current employment status and experience. By widening their horizons, you may open doors of opportunity for them that they may not have considered.

Also, make sure the information you are providing them with is accurate. For example, if you ever take a communication class and the instructor quotes the Albert Mehrabian study that shows that only 7% of our communication is verbal – RUN! That study was disproved years ago, even by Mehrabian himself, and yet trainers continue to teach it anyway.

How can you update your training programs?

_____

_____

_____

_____

_____

_____

_____

Expand your search for talent.

Because of the war for talent that is raging (and talent is winning), manufacturers cannot afford to wait until prospective employees finish school. You need to start as early in the process as possible.

The problem is that manufacturing is not always seen as an attractive career path. Prospects may the industry layoffs and worker concessions their parents experience during the economic downturn. Because of these memories, they may not feel manufacturing is a safe place to build their career.

By reaching out to students at the high school, vocational school, and college levels, manufacturers can help to reverse the negative view of jobs in the trades. They can also beat their competitors to the punch by acting early.

By identifying potential employees before they officially enter the workforce, you can create a positive image of your company as a desirable place to work.

Action Ideas:

1. Sponsor talented students who are still in school with the financial support they need to be able to continue their studies.

2. Invite students to visit your facility and work together in teams on a technical project.

3. Broadcast the benefits of working in a plant on the annual "Manufacturing Day" and beyond.

Offer formal education opportunities.

Give your employees tuition reimbursement and encourage them to complete their college degree. Although most employees appreciate any help they can get in paying for school, this benefit is especially popular with millennials.

According to a Fortune Magazine article on providing unlimited tuition reimbursement, a survey by EdAssist discovered that "if asked to choose between similar jobs, nearly 60% of respondents would pick the job with strong potential for professional development over one with regular pay raises. One in two millennials said they expected an employer's financial support in paying for further education."

Action Ideas:

1. Pay for employees to take classes towards their degree, whether or not the class has anything to do with his/her job.

2. Share your career story with your team members so they can understand how you got to where you are in your career. Telling them of your own trials and tribulations may inspire them not to give up on their dreams.

3. Celebrate your employee's graduation with public acknowledgment and a party. They worked hard for this achievement and deserve your recognition of their efforts.

Utilize YouTube videos for
employee inspiration.

SnackNation, a snack delivery service, holds "Sensei Sessions" every Monday at noon. During these meetings, the CEO shares updates and then gives the staff the time to share something they are passionate about.

Topics during these sessions include "personal development, goal setting, nutrition, or productivity hacking, and almost all of them include a motivational video clip." Your employees are watching videos anyway, and with countless hours of new content being uploaded every minute online, having the chance to narrow down the selection of what to watch may be just the inspiration your team needs.

Action Ideas:

1. Choose a theme for the meeting and let your employees pick videos that align with that topic. Give a time limit, so you can either watch shorter videos, or the team members can share the most powerful segment.

2. Kick off each of your meetings with an inspirational video. It will set the tone for the rest of your time together.

3. Want to go beyond using other people's videos? Involve your employees in the creation of a YouTube video. Get all departments involved and have some fun with it. Who knows, it may go viral.

PART 3

APPLAUD, ACKNOWLEDGE AND APPRECIATE Your Employees' Efforts and Contributions

"People work for money but go the extra mile for recognition, praise and rewards." --Dale Carnegie

Catch your employees doing their job well.

After a program, one of the participants approached me and said, "When I do something wrong, I get recognized 100% of the time. When I do something well, I rarely get noticed."

Can your employees say the same thing about the way their bosses treat them at your plant?

Marcial Losada observed teams working together in developing strategic plans. The ratio of positive to negative expressions was 6:1 for high performing teams, 3:1 for average performing teams – which is barely surviving, and .3:1 for low performing teams. In other words, low performing team members hear three times as many negatives as positives. It's a reminder of the old saying, "The beatings will continue until morale improves." It doesn't work.

Remember, what gets recognized gets repeated, so be specific in your praise.

Action Ideas:

1. When you see an employee doing something well, give them a brief, detailed acknowledgment as to why it matters to you and the organization.

2. Encourage peer-to-peer recognition. Make it fun to give credit to each other.

3. Stop trying to fix what's broken. Focus on your employees' strengths and help them make the things they do well even better.

Regularly thank your staff.

Ken Blanchard of One-Minute Manager fame said, "Effective praising has to be specific. Just walking around saying 'thanks for everything' is meaningless. If you say, 'great job' to a poor performer and the same thing to a good performer, you'll sound ridiculous to the poor performer and will demotivate the good performer."

Let your staff know that you appreciate them as both a person and a worker. Also, make sure that when you are thanking people, you mean it.

It's in the specificity of the words that you use. Exactly what did the employee do that is worth noting? Give as many details as you can. Your staff will quickly realize that you are paying attention to the good that they do – and not just the bad.

Action Ideas:

1. Say "thank you" early and often. When you hear a "thank you" from someone else, instead of saying "No problem" or "It was nothing," say, "You're welcome" or "My pleasure."

2. Keep track of your employees' successes. Your list makes performance reviews easier and more pleasant.

3. Don't wait for someone to have to "go above and beyond" to recognize them. When someone is doing better than THEY normally do, make sure to acknowledge them based on their past actions.

Understand the "why."

When employees don't understand the role they play in your company's mission, they are more likely to become disengaged. What differences does your product or service make in the world?

Here's one of my favorite parables about the importance of having a mission.

A man asked three bricklayers what they did for a living. The first replied, "I'm laying bricks." The second answered, "I'm putting up a wall." The third responded with pride in his voice, "I'm building a cathedral."

Food for thought: are your employees laying bricks, putting up walls, or building a cathedral?

Action Ideas:

1. Get down to the basic "Whys" in your business. NY Times Best-selling author, Simon Sinek said it best, "People don't buy what you do, they buy why you do what you do."

2. Share examples of how your products/services make a difference for the greater good.

3. Ask your employees why they do what they do for your company. Pay attention to their answers.

Give your branded merchandise to your team.

Your customers may or may not appreciate your branded apparel – but your employees will. Think about creating a "Welcome Basket" for your new hires. Provide company merchandise to the people who are proudest to wear it.

Presenting clients with logoed merchandise is a nice gesture, but they are not going to have the same appreciation of that brand that your employees will.

Don't make your employees buy the merchandise. Either give it to them or provide them with an allowance to choose what they would like to have. If they want to pick something out for a family member, let them. Why would you not want your employees' families to love the fact that they work for you?

Every year my husband's company gives each team member a branded t-shirt. It's always fun to see the annual design, and he now has quite the collection. From an engagement standpoint, a specially designed t-shirt is an inexpensive way to connect.

What kinds of merchandise would your team most like to receive?

_____

_____

_____

Express your gratitude.

Employees who believe their managers appreciate their work have an improved sense of worth to the organization. They also work harder and contribute more to the bottom line.

If you're thinking, "Why should I thank my staff? Isn't that what a paycheck is for?" you're missing the point. Employees who don't feel appreciated will work just hard enough not to get fired because you are probably paying them just enough so they don't quit. It's an even balance. Want your employees to give you their blood, sweat, and tears? Thank them when they do a good job. Look to catch them doing things well.

Pay attention to those "Steady Eddies" – the people that are not necessarily your rock stars, nor are they your problem children. They just show up, do the work, and go home. You may be the first person in "Eddie's" career to notice the excellent job he is doing. He'll then decide that he would like more of that, so you'll see a positive change. You won't notice if you don't do it.

What are some ways that you can thank your team?

_____

_____

_____

_____

Ask for positive workplace attributes.

Keep a running list of their positive comments and share these remarks with potential hires. You can also ask your staff what they would change if given a chance. In cases where you can modify and improve their circumstances, go ahead and do it.

When your staff knows you are listening to them, they are more likely to be engaged, which increases your retention levels. By focusing on the positives and what is working, your employees will realize that they have it pretty good. They will be less likely to fall prey to "the grass is greener over there" syndrome.

With a shrinking pool of qualified talent available to hire, it's important that you find out early if problems are brewing. Don't wait until your employee tells you they are leaving before you act.

Here are some specific questions to get started:

1. If you were in charge, what changes would you make?

2. What do you hear from your clients about our company?

3. What do you like best about working here?

4. What don't you enjoy doing? Why?

5. What other areas are you interested in pursuing?

6. How can I help you reach your goals / become more successful?

Schedule time for a meal with individual employees.

When you break bread with the people you work with, you learn a lot about each other, develop friendships, and have real conversations. Spending time with individuals or small groups can create a real connection between you and the members of your staff.

Sharing a meal is not always possible when you have lots of employees working various shifts and dealing with complicated production schedules. Do the best you can with what you have.

Getting out of the office gives you time to refresh. It sets the example that the lunch break is just that – a break from work. As your colleague or subordinate where THEY prefer to go for lunch – and go. Don't complain or make up excuses. Get out of your comfort zone and try something new. When you show that you're open to new ideas, your openness will reflect positively on you.

1. Make a goal to have a meal with each of your direct reports at least once this year.

2. Set the example for other managers to also connect during a lunch with their team members.

3. Stick to a reasonable budget for food, and let employees know what it is so that they can choose the location accordingly. By doing this, you will establish a sense of fairness and equal treatment amongst team members.

Shape up or ship out your disrespectful managers.

High turnover in a department or during a shift may be a sign that it's the manager who needs to go. Your leadership team should reflect the type of culture you want for your plant.

Incorporate 360-degree reviews and keep the feedback anonymous so that employees share what they think. When managers know that their employees have a say in whether they stay or go, they may consider their treatment of employees more carefully.

You may not like every person that works for you, but you must show them respect. If you can't be nice, at least be neutral.

Action Ideas:

1. Offer leadership development programs to ensure your leaders know the proper care and handling of employees.

2. Model best practices. Look for managers who are doing well and use their strategies to benchmark the rest of the team.

3. Document, document, document! To remove a manager who is unable or unwilling to change their tactics, make sure you can show, in writing, that you have done everything possible to rehabilitate them. You may have to prove that you had no choice but to fire them. This proper documentation will save you from a wrongful termination lawsuit...

Celebrate special occasions.

For an employee's major milestone anniversary, why not hire a limo to pick them up for work? Give them some sort of VIP treatment on their significant day. Pay attention to the things they like, and plan their day accordingly. Keep in mind that some employees like public recognition more than others.

Another way to recognize anniversaries is to offer the employee a menu of choices. Options may include: lunch with a C-Suite Executive or with their manager; leaving an hour early, or having a longer lunch; getting a chair massage (from a paid masseur, of course), receive a unique company logoed item. Be creative and put together a list that works for you and your budget.

What are some creative ways you can recognize your team members' significant milestones?

_____

_____

_____

_____

_____

_____

_____

Small rewards = Big smiles.

A client wanted to do something special for all her engineers during "Engineer's Week." Although Patty was looking for a "one-size-fits-all" approach, she realized that she could serve her team better if she put together a gift bag containing the specific things that each member likes.

She started by sending out an interest survey and then took the time to personalize and assemble individualized gift bags. The engineers were thrilled with the personal attention she spent on each gift. There wasn't a lot of money involved in the process; it was the attention to detail that mattered.

When you treat your employees as individuals and pay attention to their likes and dislikes, they will return the favor by putting their best efforts forward.

Action Ideas:

1. Create a survey to find out your employees' favorite things. Include small, medium and large items – from candy to spare time activities and maybe even vacation spots.

2. If employees don't want to participate, do the best you can based on what you know.

3. Pay attention to the things that delight your employees. Look for things that make them smile and keep notes for future reference.

Reward employees for outstanding customer service.

The better you treat your employees, the better they will take care of your customers. When someone goes above and beyond, make sure you share how that employee made a difference to the customer and to your company.

When an employee receives a "kudos" letter from a customer, share their achievement with the rest of the team and with upper management. Look for opportunities to request feedback from your customers, allowing them to share the names of employees who served them well.

One example of a field that actively seeks out direct feedback opportunities is the hotel industry. Many hotels now give out business cards with Trip Advisor information on it to make it easy for their customers to share their good experiences with the world. What are some ways can adapt their process in your industry?

Action ideas:

1. Create a "kudos" wall. When you receive letters from customers, put them in a public place so the rest of your team can see them.

2. Share it up the line. Recognition from upper management motivates employees to take more opportunities to be outstanding.

3. Publicize customer service achievements by using pictures of deserving staff on the cover and throughout your company newsletter.

Acknowledge your Veterans.

U.S. businesses are primed to see an unprecedented number of service members transitioning from the military as troops are being withdrawn from overseas and the military is facing tighter budgets.

What does this mean for you? With approximately 1.5 million service members coming back into workforce in the next three to five years, you'll have opportunities to add these veterans to your staff. Hire them and make sure you honor them for their service.

When you recognize the people who have served their country, you help make their transition from military to civilian life easier. Because the military already puts great importance on formal recognition, finding ways to acknowledge them can be easy to do.

Here are a few ideas from the Michael C. Fina (MCFRecognition.com) website for honoring your veteran employees.

1. Hold a Pinning Ceremony: Gather your vets together and present them with pins that represent their branch of service.

2. Give a "Salute Package": Make Veteran's Day special by giving them a small gift, a handwritten note, and a formal certificate.

3. Increase Veteran Awareness: Ensure that your employees are aware of the veterans working for you, so they can thank your veterans for their service in their own special way.

Have an employee appreciation picnic.

Whether it's hot dogs and potato salad in the parking lot for employees only, or a full-blown company picnic with families in tow, look for ways to build friendships while having fun in a casual atmosphere.

A manufacturing client holds their annual employee picnic at a large amusement park. Each employee gets two free tickets and a discounted rate for their family members. Most employees attend, and they enjoy getting together and seeing the kids as they grow up.

They have a huge raffle at lunchtime where the leadership team rewards the winners with everything from grills to large screen TVs. The interesting thing about the lottery is that management cannot win. The primary goal is to thank and honor the hourly employees who work in the plant.

These employees work hard all year, and this picnic is just one of the many ways that management thanks them for their contributions.

What are some ideas that you can use to host an employee appreciation picnic?

_____

_____

_____

_____

_____

Send birthday cards with gift cards enclosed.

How do you know which gift cards to include? Ask? What is your favorite coffee shop, restaurant, or service that has a gift card you can purchase? Your employee may not remember telling you their choice, but when they open the card, they will see that you care enough to pay attention.

Most grocery stores and other retail outlets offer a wide variety of gift cards. It's no longer necessary to go to one store and buy a stack of cards to dole out. Make it personal.

Have the card signed by management with a personal note, thanking them individually for what they do to make a difference in the company. The more specific, the better.

You don't have to spend a lot of money to make someone's day. It really is the thought – the sincere, authentic, caring thought – that counts.

Action Ideas:

1. Use Survey Monkey or another online tool to find out your employees' favorite things.

2. Choose or create personalized cards that will mean something to their recipient.

3. Give your managers a "birthday budget" to work with – and make sure they use it in full.

Let your leaders serve your team.

Yes, cash is a great way to reward your employees. Unfortunately, the cash "high" is short-lived. Money is not a long-term motivator. Using money in conjunction with other incentives can be a great way to reward and motivate employees. By being creative, you'll find plenty of free and low-cost ways to engage with your workers.

You want to connect with staff in a more personal way than cash. In doing so, you'll increase your team's loyalty, work ethic, and productivity.

Why not have a contest where the prizes include being served by the company leaders? Maybe your managers can serve lunch, wash employees' cars, or make a gourmet coffee run. Let your imagination run wild.

Action Ideas:

1. Provide a catered breakfast and have your leadership team serve your employees.

2. Have a contest where the prize is having the employee's car washed by their manager in the parking lot.

3. Set up a dunking machine in your company parking lot. Have you and the rest of your management team sit in the tank and let your employees have at it. The game is a fun way to show that you're willing to have some fun at your expense for the good of the team.

Give tangible recognition daily.

Reinforcing good behavior must consistently happen if it is to be meaningful. By using tangible recognition practices every day, you'll reinforce the positive actions of your workers and create a culture of recognition within your plant.

If you spot a worker cleaning up a mess that someone else made, why not hand him/her a "Kudos Card" for their part in making the workplace a bit nicer/safer? No, I'm not saying that you need to hand out a reward every time an employee does something nice for another. However, it only takes a few occasions for other employees to notice that their managers are paying attention to the good that they do.

Designing and printing a reward card is a great way to supplement a more formal recognition program. You can create additional cards for employees to recognize their peers. Then, each quarter, have a raffle with prizes drawn from the cards received. Use your imagination and maximize the fun.

Ideas for designing a reward card and process for using them:

_____

_____

_____

_____

_____

Write it down.

When you tell someone you appreciate them, you create a great memory; when you write it down, you create a treasure. Give your workers tangible evidence of a job well done.

Whether you scribble "You Rock!" on a Post-It note, write a thank you note, or compose a letter of appreciation, make sure to put it in writing. If you're wondering the difference between the last two – (in the author's opinion) a thank you note is for something specific while a letter of appreciation shows how the recipient makes a difference every day.

You can also give these appreciation letters to employees who went through a tough time and came out shining. Take the time to notice their successful comeback. Giving this type of approbation shows tremendous support of the employees who help you.

1. Purchase a photo frame with a voice recorder in it. Place a certificate of appreciation inside, and include a personally recorded message of appreciation.

2. Record a brief video on your phone, embedded in an email or using a webinar service thanking your employee "in person." Make it short, personalized, and unexpected. You'll make their day.

3. When you write a handwritten note to a team member, include a copy in their personnel file.

Use gift cards instead of cash rewards.

Give your managers a variety of gift cards that they can hand out when they catch their employees going above and beyond at work. To make the exchange even more powerful, have the manager include a note as to the reason WHY the employee deserves this token of appreciation. The gift card will get used, and the letter will be treasured.

One of the main reasons that gift cards are more compelling than cash is the staying power of physical rewards. Cash gets used to pay bills or put in the bank. Most employees don't even remember how used their cash prize. If they purchased something with a gift card, they will have a pleasant memory of the giver each time they use what they bought.

Yes, you do have to pay attention to the tax implications of gift cards. Even smaller denomination cards have value, and you want to make sure you stay out of legal trouble when you're using these cards.

Action Ideas:

1. Find out what our employees' favorite gift card is. Don't assume that everyone enjoys coffee.

2. Keep the amount nominal. It's not about the money; it's acknowledging a job well done.

3. Make sure that your managers give out ALL their allotted cards. Make sure that your managers are focusing on catching employees in the act of doing something well.

PART 4

NURTURE and Empower Your Team

"As you navigate through the rest of your life, be open to collaboration. Other people and other people's ideas are often better than your own. Find a group of people who challenge and inspire you, spend a lot of time with them, and it will change your life." ~ *Amy Poehler*

Give power to the people.

When empowering frontline factory workers, managers may have more latitude than they realize. It's true. You don't always have the power to change pay, increase benefits or modify company policies on a whim, but you can empower your employees in a variety of ways.

Here are a few ideas:

1. **Communicate openly**. Keep your staff in the loop and let them know what's happening in the organization

2. **Give employees a voice**. At Toyota, if line worker sees a problem with a car, he/she has the power to stop the entire assembly line until the issue is fixed.

3. **Maintain good relations with the union**. Stop with the "us versus them" attitude. Even in the heat of negotiations, keep a respectful composure.

4. **Address tensions between tenured and newer employees.** Don't let complaints fester.

5. **Show support for career development**. If an employee is looking for ways to enhance their career, provide them with options and a plan for career development.

Given the diminishing number of people coming into manufacturing as a career, staff retention is vital for the long-term success of your plant.

Offer a challenging yet supportive work environment.

When you give your employees challenging tasks, you boost their creativity, productivity, and overall profitability. Why not look for jobs that are currently being done by supervisors and assign them to subordinates who are ready and willing to take on the assignments. You will increase visibility at the lower ranks and potentially determine your future leaders.

By challenging your workers, you may uncover their hidden strengths. You gain the benefit of using current staff to fill upcoming leadership roles, making your succession planning more fruitful. Hiring from the outside has its share of challenges, so why not take advantage of your homegrown talent who knows your company inside and out.

Action Ideas:

1. Encourage friendly competition between departments to see how everyone can make your products/processes better.

2. Assign employees to manage projects that stretch their abilities and require them to learn something new.

3. Delegate without dumping. Give employees the authority to make the decisions they need to make to complete the task successfully.

Encourage prudent risks.

When you provide a safe environment for innovative thinking, you'll grow faster than companies who refuse to "fix what's not broken."

An excellent way to encourage risk is to use "Get Out of Jail Free" cards. Employees can use these if they want to try something that involves a risk. By handing out these cards, leaders demonstrate that they value risk taking. They assure staff that they have their back if the worker needs them.

Think about it, some of your best money-saving/making ideas may come from sources you never considered. If something goes wrong, learn from the lesson and move on.

In his Entrepreneur Magazine article, "3 Ways Companies Can Encourage Smart Risk Taking," Salim Ismail shares three action ideas:

1. "Resist the urge to say no." To protect your organization from risk aversion, start with "yes and."

2. "Never stop experimenting." To join execution and innovation, put our own set of experimentation processes in place.

3. "Reward insightful experiments." When your team is operating within strategic, commercial, ethical and legal frameworks and they avoid re-creating old mistakes, celebrate the failures that their willingness to experiment created.

Add meaning to work.

Every worker has different motivations. If you look at Maslow's hierarchy of needs, you'll find that many hourly employees stay at the first two levels and simply meet their physiological and safety needs. They don't strive for the higher levels (Love/belonging; Esteem; Self-Actualization) to reach their full potential, either at home or work.

Research done on factory workers finds that three core values are important in their lives: meaning, dignity, and self-determination. Understanding these insights is key to increasing engagement.

Meaning: They want to feel that their contribution is valuable to the organization.

Dignity: They want management to treat them with respect.

Self-determination: They want to have a sense of control and ownership in how they do their work.

How can you make sure you employees' core values are being met?

_____

_____

_____

_____

_____

_____

Ask employees to create new ways to complete tasks.

Assemble an employee "think tank" and assign them a specific problem. See how many ideas they can come up with to solve the issue. Challenge them from a low-budget or no-budget standpoint to encourage creativity.

When brainstorming ideas, make sure that the goals of the project are understood. The team members need to be able to measure the progress of their plan compared to what is currently in place. Employees should have control over achieving their goal. Finally, remember to include a reward system when the team meets their goals.

To add even more fun to the process, have a recognition ceremony for the best ideas of the year. Come up with different categories of awards and several nominees in each category so you can open the envelope and announce the winner – just like your own "Idea Oscars."

Action Ideas:

1. Provide "Mind Mapper" or similar software for employees to capture their thoughts legibly.

2. Give members of each team the opportunity to present their concepts to leadership and get feedback on their ideas.

3. Let the team, and the rest of the company, know when you implemented one of their ideas and update them on the successful results of their designs.

Create an Employee Experience Committee.

Empower your staff to make the changes they would ideally like to see in the workplace. Assemble a team whose sole purpose is finding ways to improve culture and engagement. Give team members access to management to share their findings.

Even the US Department of Commerce is looking to increase engagement with their own Employee Engagement Team. Their Mission "is to create an environment that values and supports employee engagement and promotes a healthy organization by developing internal programs and events for employees."

Their vision: "We envision an organization composed of dedicated leaders and employees who are committed to organizational success and job satisfaction."

An Employee Experience Committee will:

1. Measure current levels of engagement.

2. Solicit ideas and feedback from employees on how to increase their engagement.

3. Put together a plan for resources needed.

4. Share findings with management.

5. Follow up, review, and revise as necessary.

* Note to management: Act on your employees' suggestions. Let your workers know who suggested each idea and how you implemented it.

Share the greater mission.

When you have a well-defined vision, it's easier to make sure your employees share your company's values.

Getting the right people "on the bus" is critical to having a company culture that works. Take an honest look at the people you have working for you. Are they still a fit for your business, or have you outgrown them Are the people in the company in the right position or would their skills be better utilized elsewhere?

One example of a company that really defines its culture is Zappos. Check out their Ten Core Values:

- "Deliver WOW Through Service
- Embrace and Drive Change
- Create Fun and A Little Weirdness
- Be Adventurous, Creative, and Open-Minded
- Pursue Growth and Learning
- Build Open and Honest Relationships with Communication
- Build a Positive Team and Family Spirit
- Do More with Less
- Be Passionate and Determined
- Be Humble"

Circle your favorite(s). How will you implement them with your team?

_____

_____

Give back.

Millennial and Gen Z employees want to work for organizations that are serving a mission that is greater than themselves. Empower your employees to choose a cause(s) they'd like to support outside of the workplace. Then let them do it.

Back in the day, there were limited charities from which to choose. Now you'll find an agency for every type of need. There are apps! For example, CauseCast.com lets your employees choose the charities they most care about, so they are more likely to get involved.

By allowing employees occasional time off work to serve – once a quarter, twice a year, annually – whatever works best for your company – you'll invigorate your team with a renewed sense of purpose.

Action Ideas:

1. Want to know what charities are important to your workers? Ask!

2. Model the behavior you want to see. If you are asking your employees to volunteer, make sure you are doing the same.

3. Look for opportunities (Habitat for Humanity for example) that groups of employees can volunteer for at the same time. You'll build stronger relationships and friendships outside of the workplace.

Make your employees use their paid time off.

If you have employees who are proud of the fact that they "haven't taken a vacation in years," you need to change their attitude.

There are way too many workers who don't use any or all their vacation time. They either think their manager will allow the time off, or they're afraid that their coworkers will view them as a slacker.

Vacations refresh and energize your employees. In fact, employees usually get a lot of work done before leaving (the "Friday before vacation" syndrome). When and then they return to work, they are likely to come back with a renewed energy and an invigorated outlook.

Action Ideas:

1. Have a "Use It or Lose It" policy for at least part of your employees' vacation time. People want to save time for a special occasion, but often that "special time" never comes.

2. Take advantage of technology and let your employees work from home when they are not feeling well or need a "mental health day." You'll keep the rest of the office from getting sick as well.

3. Cross-train across departments so employees can easily fill in for their coworkers while they are on vacation. If you're still short of available workers, hire more people or bring in temps.

Build an employee-generated list of FAQs.

Because your employee handbook only goes so far in addressing everyday situations, let your employees help. Because they are on the front lines every day serving your customers and working with each other, ask them to write down their most frequently asked questions (FAQs).

By using these kinds of real-world examples, you will be better equipped to define what works, and what doesn't work in your company culture.

Action Ideas:

1. Have a "Situation of the Week" contest. Address questions like "What did you do when the production line went down?" or "What if a buyer wants something we can't deliver?" Share the answers so everyone can see the different ways of looking at these situations.

2. Pay attention to questions that you get from new employees. If you notice specific issues that come up on a regular basis, put together a procedure for handling them. This extra effort can help you in your customer service training as well as furthering your new hire onboarding process.

3. Compile the Q&A on your company intranet or newsletter. Recognize employees for their creativity in effectively handling questions and providing appropriate answers.

Discuss career development plans.

Do this at least twice a year – and follow up to help employees achieve their goals. Some of the best questions to ask your team members include, "What keeps you here?" "What can we do better to help?" and "What would cause you to leave?" The last two can be a little scary to ask, ask them anyway.

Research shows that companies that invest in their employees' career development reduce the risk of losing their most valuable employees to the competition. Plus, it's one of the things job applicants are putting a priority on receiving.

By providing an identifiable career path, along with coaching and mentoring high potential employees, you are giving your team members what they need to move into new roles within the organization over time.

Action Ideas:

1. Highlight employee success stories for real world examples of how to make progress through the organization

2. Encourage your managers to sit down with their staff to find out the specifics of their career aspirations. Put together a plan to help them achieve their objectives.

3. Make sure that each employee specifically knows what they need to do to move to the next level in their career. Do they need to take a certificate class? Finish their degree? Attend a training program? Tell them.

Demonstrate that you trust your people.

Allow workers to acquire what they need to do their jobs without having to jump through a lot of hoops to get it. Don't insist on approving every minute detail of a project. Trust that your employees have the experience, knowledge, and competence to handle the particulars of a project without constant oversight.

Managers who rule with an iron first – micromanaging, rigid control and negativity, create a climate of anxiety and fear. Although an autocratic management style may bring you a well-behaved workforce, it certainly won't encourage employees to bring up ideas or share potential problem areas. Give your staff the authority they need to act on their own.

Action ideas:

1. Delegate responsibilities. Give your employees broad responsibilities for executing a task or project.

2. Convey clear expectations. Don't make your employees guess the desired outcome.

3. Allow for flexibility in work schedules. Maybe permitting occasional telecommuting is an option. Does flex-time or job sharing make sense? Talk to your employees to find out what works best for them.

4. Banish unnecessary hierarchy. Give team members the latitude they need to approach management with their ideas and suggestions for better customer service.

Offer opportunities for job-sharing or cross-training.

With 10,000 Baby Boomers retiring every day, it's essential to have the workforce you need to get the job done. Cross training not only adds depth and variety to your employees' skill level, but it also allows your management team to leverage the talent and expertise you already have in house.

If you're finding your employees are disengaged, cross-training may re-ignite their spark and passion by giving them stimulating work to do. When you expose your staff to other jobs within the plant, they feel a sense of growth and accomplishment while learning something new.

You can also use cross training as a substitute for using temporary workers. Your employees may travel between departments, but their understanding of the company's processes and value continues to expand.

Action Ideas:

1. Ask what they want. Let staff members identify the jobs they would like to learn and give them the chance to try it out.

2. Put together a program. A formal job rotation program gives everyone the opportunity to try something new.

3. Collect feedback. Ask employees what they like about the program and any areas they would improve.

Learn lessons from each failure.

In Liz Ryan's "Five Lessons Only Failure Can Teach You" article in *Forbes Magazine*, she shares these five lessons learned from making mistakes.

1. "How to back up and reflect." What went wrong and how can you prevent that from happening again?

2. "How to fix something that breaks." You now have a new skill and are better prepared for future events.

3. "How to soften the energy." When you stop being defensive and open up to yourself and others about what went wrong, you feel better.

4. "How to set intention." Make a personal commitment to yourself to get the task done and realize that you may get distracted along the way.

5. "How to make a mistake and keep going." What doesn't kill you makes you stronger. Learn your lesson, let it go, and move on.

What is a lesson you've learned from a failure?

_____

_____

_____

_____

_____

_____

Acknowledge employee aspirations.

Account for both the personal and career interests of your employees. By focusing on the whole person and not just what they do at work, your shop will get more value from your workers.

For example, if an employee mentions that they have always enjoyed teaching, but he or she doesn't have any training responsibilities, look for ways to get them engaged in coaching or mentoring others. How do you find out what your employees' goals are? Ask them.

A textile manufacturing client went so far as to hire a dream manager to help connect their employees to their aspirations. This company supported their employees in creating a pie-baking business, a financial training program (that they also used in-house), and other business ventures. Give your employees time to process your sincerity in asking. They way to trust you are taking them and their ideas seriously.

Action Ideas:

1. Ask your team members, "What can we do to help you achieve your goals?"

2. Encourage your employee to make a shared commitment to creating a win/win for them and your company.

3. Provide opportunities to let your employees share their newly developed skills within the organization.

Provide self-care opportunities for employees.

Chronic work-related stress is taking a toll on your plant's productivity. Research estimates that losses associated with stress cost US business $300 billion each year. What can you do?

Encourage self-care. When you help your employees make better lifestyle choices, you'll reduce your absenteeism, turnover, and health care costs, while boosting your throughput in the process.

Here are a few ideas to get you started:

Exercise. There are many physical and mental benefits to physical activity. Provide gym memberships or build a workout center. Give incentives to employees who walk, run, or bike to work instead of driving.

Promote healthy eating. If you're providing lunch or snacks during the day, bring in nutritious options. Holding a health fair will educate employees how to make better choices in what they eat.

Encourage quitting smoking. Because smoking reduces focus and concentration, it impairs productivity. Include a tobacco cessation program in your benefits. Your insurance rates may go down as well – bonus!

Mindfulness practices. Holding yoga classes during lunch is probably not an option for most factories. Instead, host stress reduction or mindfulness training programs several times during a day to cover all shifts.

PART 5

Getting to KNOW Your People

"Great things in business are never done by one person.
They're done by a team of people." ~ Steve Jobs

Welcome new hires with flair.

Put together a welcome committee to enthusiastically greet new hires. Provide a plant tour and a welcome packet filled with information about local restaurants, best local bars, branded merchandise, etc.

Your welcome committee may consist of staff from different departments and shifts. The benefit for committee members is that they get a nice break from their routine. It also connects your tenured employees with their new coworkers from day one.

Give new hires a VIP badge to show that they are a valuable addition to your organization. Assign a lunch buddy to introduce them around and connect them with as many potential new friends as possible.

Remember, your new employee went on several interviews before accepting your position. Don't make it easy for another company to woo them away. Create an experience that makes them want to stay.

Action Ideas:

1. Start welcoming the new hire before their first day on the job. Keep in touch before their start date.

2. Send a handwritten note, letting the new person know that you are looking forward to working with them.

3. Put together an org chart with fellow team members' pictures on it so they can get familiar with the people they will be working with.

Understand personality styles.

Personality assessments are great tools to help staff understand each other better, and their use may improve the communication process. DISC is the assessment that I use most often, but there are numerous tests available.

Managers don't necessarily have to agree with, or even to like their employees, but they MUST be polite. It is the leader's job to figure out how to work most effectively with their team.

To get the process started, have everyone take the assessment. Follow up with discussions or team building activities that allow different groups to learn about each other. When employees understand themselves and their colleagues, it creates more harmony. When it comes to employee engagement, it's not about "treating others the way YOU like to be treated," but rather it is about treating others "the way THEY want to be treated."

Reasons to incorporate personality assessments:

1. Employees have a better understanding of themselves and each other.

2. You'll get the right person in the right position based on their style, attitude, and aptitude.

3. You'll create a more balanced team. Having all four personality styles on a team brings about different perspectives and approaches to problem-solving.

Implement a leadership outreach program.

Find out what's happening in your company by scheduling face time with your hourly employees. Caution: before starting, let your employees know what you're doing and why you're doing it. Tell your staff that you value their input and that you will be scheduling conversations with each of them.

If you don't pre-call your intentions, employees may be suspicious or think that they are in trouble. Keep in mind that the first couple employees who you invite for a sit-down may be wary of telling you the truth. Create an environment of trust so that, no matter what they say, you take it at face value.

Remember, their perspective is their reality. No, your workers probably don't know the whole story. No, your staff doesn't understand your situation and what you're going through, listen to what they have to say.

All that matters is that you create a safe place for your employees to share, in their view, what is already good and what you can do to improve the company.

How can I create connections with my employees?

_____

_____

_____

_____

Encourage peer-to-peer recognition.

You know how important it is to show your workers how much you value them. But, receiving kudos from a coworker goes a long way in creating a highly engaged workforce.

By focusing on peer-to-peer recognition, you create a natural accountability system, as employees look for ways they can help each other without feeling that they are "sucking up" to management.

Peer to peer recognition also helps in performance appraisals because employees soon learn that they can't act one way in front of their managers and another way in front of their peers.

Make the recognition fun, low-cost, and abundant. Don't limit employees' opportunities to recognize and appreciate each other. The more the better!

Action Ideas:

1. Get the word out. Let your employees know who is being recognized and why. Give staff a chance to recognize and support the kudos.

2. Be consistent. Make sure that employees know when and where they can expect to learn about the accomplishments of others – meetings, company newsletter, intranet, etc.

3. Be creative. Empower your team members to recognize each other in different ways to keep it interesting.

Start a referral program.

Encourage your staff for recommendations to fill open positions. You will get better hires when your employees refer people they know, like, and trust.

One plant manager shared that he encourages his staff to post job openings on their personal Facebook pages. This strategy works because it is usually their best team members who are doing the posting. Gallup research shows that highly engagement people have a "best friend" at work. It's in your company's interest to let those friendships happen.

The chances are good that if workers like their job, they are engaged and productive. If they are engaged and productive, workers will self-select the people who they know will be a good fit for the organization.

If you pay referral fees, keep the amount modest, but worth the effort. You don't want to encourage people to recommend their people for the cash alone; there needs to be more to it than that.

Ideas to start an employee referral program:

_____

_____

_____

_____

_____

Establish a "buddy system."

Encourage your seasoned employees to mentor your newer staff members. You will benefit by retaining the knowledge and experience of your tenured employees and help them to feel relevant. The newer employees will learn from someone who has been in the trenches and knows how to do the job.

Mentorship is a terrific way to create connections between the different generations in the workplace, thus enhancing your succession planning efforts.

Make sure you're teaming up people who are compatible and be okay if the first pairing doesn't work out. The goal is to create relationships and friendships on the job, thereby engaging both your new and your long-term staff members by letting them bond with each other.

Action Ideas:

1. **Train your mentors**. Let them know what their role encompasses and how to set boundaries with their mentee.

2. **Set up a time frame**. Establish the length of the commitment and a minimum number of meetings that the mentor and mentee will have.

3. **Measure success**. Look for increased job satisfaction and reduced turnover as evidence of a successful mentoring program.

Share the personal side of life.

Highly engaged management teams recognize that their staff is likely to be more engaged and productive when they bring their authentic selves to work. Allowing employees to share portions of their personal life creates a solid basis for connection.

When you offer opportunities for your staff to know each other personally AND professionally, you allow relationships to form. Gallup research shows that when an employee has a "best friend" at work, they are likely to be more engaged and less likely to leave.

Action Ideas:

1. You may already have a "Bring your child to work day," why not try a "Bring your pet" to work day. As long as pets are well behaved, your employees and their pets may enjoy the extra time together.

2. Have a periodic "Show and Tell" where employees bring in something from home and tell their colleagues about it. As they share their hobbies, awards, collections, and other interests, you'll encourage people to connect based on mutual interests.

3. Give employees the opportunity to share a cause or charity they support. Allow them to post information on their favorite charity so your team can become better educated on the many causes they may choose to help.

Hold friendly competitions.

There are many ways to get employees involved in friendly contests. Host a variety of events, so you can get many of the staff involved as possible in the things they like best.

Pinterest.com has lots of ideas that you can use. With the number of "Pinterest Fail" sites, you can offer prizes for the best representation of a Pinterest idea as well as the funniest "fail."

Host a chili or BBQ cook-off or a brownie bake-off. Make sure the entries are anonymous, so it's fair for everyone. Encourage participants to bring in their "secret sauce" recipe and let the judging begin.

You don't necessarily have to give a cash prize – bragging rights or a plastic gold trophy still give competitors a good incentive to win.

Ideas for intra-company competitions:

_____

_____

_____

_____

_____

_____

_____

_____

Allow employees to switch jobs with each other.

When employees know and are comfortable with each other's jobs, it helps them be more productive and efficient workers. Having more qualified staff to choose from, also helps improve the scheduling process in the plant.

It's important to keep the lines of communication open between workers and managers to ensure that they are adequately covering the production schedules.

By fostering a culture of collaboration, your team will learn how they are all working toward a common goal. When employees take pride in being able to do their job as well as the job of others, they feel a greater sense of accomplishment in their ability. They will live up to the standards that you set for them and create the type of culture you want.

Action Ideas:

1. Ask for team members to volunteer to take on available shifts, so you develop a self-sufficient team.

2. Minimize confusion by managing shift changes. Encourage open and honest feedback about your staff's needs and desires.

3. Formally cross-train your team members, so you know they are doing the job correctly.

Use Icebreakers to get to know your team.

The Gallup Q12 is a list of statements that organizations can use to determine if their employees are engaged. One of the declarations is "I have a best friend at work." Icebreaking activities are a great way to help employees get to know each other personally and let the friendships begin.

You read earlier in this book about "Two Truths and a Lie." Here are a few more icebreakers to try:

1. **My Three Shining Moments** – Each person shares three significant moments from their life. These events may be personal or professional. Debrief it by finding the common threads in the highlights mentioned.

2. **My Favorite Things** – Pick a general topic (movies, TV shows, music) and have participants share what their favorite thing is and why. Debrief it by having people share what they learned about each other.

3. **Five of Anything** – Have attendees brainstorm five ideas about the meeting topic. For example, if you're meeting to discuss employee retention, have members come up with five things that cause them to stay at their job.

Creativity is encouraged, but keep it rated "G." Icebreakers help you learn things about others that don't come up in regular workplace conversation, thereby creating additional opportunities to connect.

PART 6

SERVE others to create an awesome culture

"Work and live to serve others, to leave the world a little better than you found it and garner for yourself as much peace of mind as you can. This is happiness." ~David Sarnoff

Have fewer meetings.

Face it, unless there's food, no one enjoys going to the time-suck event known as a meeting. Yes, it is important for everyone to find out what's going on. However, most of the time, sharing specific updates is just as effective.

When you do need to meet, have an agenda, a hard start, and a hard stop. Ask for input and stick to the schedule. Respect your employees' time and give them the opportunity to plan their day efficiently.

Even though you would love to, you are not going to eliminate all meetings. Often, you can reformat your meetings to avoid the time-wasting aspects and get a lot more done. Your team members should feel energized rather than exhausted at the end of your time together.

Action Ideas:

1. Have a hard start and hard stop. If it's not on the agenda, it doesn't get discussed. Invite only those people who need to be present, and allow them to leave when they are done.

2. Have smaller, shorter meetings and hold people accountable for tasks assigned.

3. Have stand-up meetings before each shift so outgoing workers can share status updates with the incoming shift employees and supervisors. Keep the sessions short – five to fifteen minutes is ideal.

Make up your own holiday.

Break up the blandness of uniforms and office attire by having a theme day where you encourage employees to dress up for the occasion. Whether you choose Halloween, the eighties, or the first day of Spring, let your employees have some fun. Setting up a photo booth for group pictures is a terrific way to capture the moment.

Hold a desk or department decorating contest and give the winners a small prize. You can choose a theme or let each group choose their own. You'll create a sense of camaraderie and can use this as a team building activity.

Keep it simple. You don't have to spend a lot of money in doing this. Encourage creativity by challenging your team members to spend as little money as possible.

To make sure employees are comfortable, no matter their belief system, you may want to stay away from traditional holidays. Use Chase's Calendar of Events, at chasescalendarofevents.com, for unique celebration ideas – or just make up your own holiday.

Unique celebrations ideas:

_____

_____

_____

_____

Offer flex time where possible.

Enable employees to determine how, where, and when they work. Focus on successful outcomes instead of the details of HOW the employees perform their jobs. Hold your team members accountable for their performance and give them the flexibility they want and deserve.

Yes, it's difficult to give up control, but what if there is a better way? Are you so focused on getting the job done YOUR way, that you close yourself off to opportunities?

Cutting down on their commute shows that you care about giving your team members their time back. Yes, there will be employees who you need to monitor to make sure they are not abusing the extra flexibility, but it is always advised to err on the side of trust.

Action Ideas:

1. Do your homework. Not all positions are conducive to non-traditional work times. The work still needs to get done.

2. Put it in writing. Make sure your policy is detailed, clear, and nondiscriminatory. Consider positions, not people when creating your plan.

3. Keep up communication. Include your flex staff in your on-site meetings, so they don't feel alienated from the rest of the team.

Start your meetings on a positive note.

Instead of jumping right into business, begin each meeting by letting employees share a bit of good news. The stories shared can be personal or business related. Keep them short and sweet, so you have time to take care of business. By starting meetings in this manner, you'll shift the energy and launch the rest of the agenda on a more forward-thinking note.

Here are a few ideas that work:

1. One of the boards I served on started each session by sharing "Thirty Seconds of Good." We went into the meeting agenda with a much more positive outlook.

2. A manufacturer put a ledger by the time clock. When employees punch in, they are encouraged to write down "one good thing." (They went through my training program, so they understood the benefits of a daily gratitude practice.)

3. At Rotary Club meetings, they have a "Happy Bucks" segment where members pay a dollar to share good news. The money collected goes to a charity the club supports, and everyone at the meeting gets to share in the celebration.

How can you create moments to share good news?

_____

_____

_____

Offer a healthy meal.

If you're bringing in lunch, set up a salad bar with a variety of vegetables, meats, and cheeses. It's not only a healthier alternative, but it satisfies everyone - especially those on a diet.

Take steps to help your employees remain happy and healthy by educating them on proper nutrition and giving them access to information and trying new things.

There's a quote that says that we spend the first half of our life using our health to get wealth and the second half of our life using our wealth to get our health back. Let's start early and provide the means for a healthy team.

Here are a few ways to offer healthy meal choices:

1. Set up a smoothie station. Have a variety of fruits, nuts, protein powders, vegetables, etc., and let employees create their own concoction. (Make sure you have one person running the machine – for convenience and safety's sake.)

2. Bring in varieties of unusual fruits so your employees can learn about them and try something they might not buy on their own.

3. Encourage your vegetarians and vegans to whip up a few of their favorite creations to demonstrate alternatives to having meat with every meal.

Expand your bereavement policy.

As the population ages, you may find more of your employees must deal with the death of a loved one. Although most policies give workers three days for immediate family, primary caregivers may need at least a week to deal with all the logistics surrounding death and burial.

If the relative lives out of state, it creates a bigger burden on the employee with limited time off. Also, employees need time to process their loss, grieve their loved one, and figure out their new normal.

If they come back too soon, they are probably not going to be very productive. It's impossible to park your grief at the door and then pick it up at five. Show compassion and give your employees the time they need to heal.

To prevent employees from taking advantage of this policy, you can require documentation. The important thing is to allow your team members to be with their family when the need for togetherness is high.

Don't make your employees choose their job over their family — nothing good comes out of that.

Ideas for expanding the current leave policy:

_____

_____

_____

Acknowledge losses appropriately.

Suffering a loss is difficult. Going through a tough time without the support of your coworkers can make a difficult situation even harder to bear.

Whether a team member loses a family member, a close friend, or a pet, acknowledge the loss in a heartfelt manner. You may find it difficult to find the right words to say, just say something.

Small gestures can have a significant impact. By expressing your concern, verbally or in writing, you show your staff that you care about them and their family. They feel supported by the entire plant.

Action Ideas:

1. Express your sympathy in person, over the phone, or in a card. Contact the employee as soon as you hear of their loss to let them know they are in your thoughts during this difficult time.

2. Offer to help with the employee's tasks at work. Send food or look for other ways to provide support for them at home.

3. Donate to a charity in their loved one's name.

4. Check in and make sure your employee is doing all right.

5. Remember that grief comes and goes as time passes. Be patient.

Focus on your staff's safety, ergonomics, comfort.

Your physical workplace environment contributes to the organization and quality of your employees' work. Physical comfort during the workday impacts employee motivation, performance, satisfaction, and engagement.

No, you don't have to buy the $2500 ergonomic chair, if the $250 model or a simple back support device will work. Investing in your employees' health and safety will also keep you out of court. Disgruntled employees like to call places like OSHA, and you don't want to be at the wrong end of their investigation.

The degree to which your team members can personalize their own workplace environment or control aspects such as lighting, temperature, and sound can make a huge difference in their motivation level.

When your workforce sees that you are paying attention to their basic needs ahead of bottom-line profits, you'll see both productivity and profits increase.

What are some of the things you can do to make your physical environment better?

_____

_____

_____

_____

Keep your head count lean

People would rather be busy than bored, so running lean will help you keep your team active and engaged throughout the workday.

The great recession of 2007 – 2009 gave many companies the opportunity to run a very tight operation to stay in business. If you must make a choice, it's better to err on the side of too few employees than too many. You want to have all your shifts covered, and have adequate backup. You also don't want to overwork and burn out your staff.

Create cross-training programs to help employees develop skills across a broad area. Not only will you have a more skilled workforce, but you'll also be able to keep employees busy when there is less demand for their primary skills. During the process, you may learn that your staff has skills that you did not know they possessed.

Action Ideas:

1. If your job descriptions are not up-to-date, the time to take care of that is now.

2. Update your job descriptions regularly. Not only will it keep you safe legally, but your employees will know what the company expects from them.

3. Ask for honest feedback on your processes and procedures. Implement suggestions and share the credit when doing so.

Offer bonus time off.

When production schedules allow, letting employees leave an hour or two early as a reward for completing a major project is very much appreciated.

The invention of the smart phone has pretty much eliminated any semblance of work/life balance that we used to have before being connected 24/7. Granting your staff the chance to recharge for a couple of hours means a lot.

A great example from my hometown was the day of the victory parade celebrating the Cleveland Cavaliers basketball championship. More than 1.25 million people packed the streets of downtown Cleveland for this historic moment. Instead of forcing their staff to come in (considering no Cleveland sports team had won ANY championship since 1964) many companies closed up shop to let their employees attend the parade.

Instead of enduring a painfully non-productive work day, companies benefited from the energy and enthusiasm of rejuvenated employees returning to work the following day.

On what occasions can you give bonus time off?

_____

_____

_____

_____

Bring in a treat.

In the summertime, bring in ice cream and have an ice cream social. In the fall, bring in apple pie. Look for ways to reward your staff with seasonal treats. Make it nice. Don't be a cheapskate – that can backfire.

For example, a client hired an ice cream truck to come to their facility and sell their employees ice cream cones for one dollar. Leaders thought that by giving employees a break and a cheap snack, they would appreciate the effort. They didn't.

Employees didn't understand why they had to pay for the ice cream. (No good deed goes unpunished, right?) If management had considered the few hundred extra dollars as an investment in their employees and a reward for the good work they do, they probably would have seen a much more grateful reaction.

A few ideas to get you started:

1. Bring in a variety of food trucks and let employees choose what and where they want to eat. You may or may not want to subsidize the purchase. Make an event out of it.

2. Have a mid-week treat in the breakroom. Waffle Wednesdays? Tuesday afternoon cookie platter? Taco Thursdays?

3. On a hot day, have managers go through the plant handing out ice cream bars. On a cold day, have them make the rounds with hot chocolate.

Show off your employees' "furry children."

Promote a "cutest pet" photo contest and let your employees vote for the winners. Give pet toys or treats for prizes. For those people who don't have pets, let them find creative ways to participate if they'd like to.

Pet photos do not have to be limited to the animals that employees currently own. Maybe there's a friend's or family member's pet they can include. Get extra creative and have a story that goes along with it, so employees can learn more about the "pet personality" that makes that pet worthy of the recognition.

Have different cat-agories (pug, I mean pun intended) such as cutest pet, silliest pet, animals in action, best costume, etc. Get creative!

What are some ways you can include your employees' "furry children" at work?

_____

_____

_____

_____

_____

_____

_____

Create a more positive workplace.

The book, "Strengths Finder" by Tom Rath shows readers why it's important to develop their strengths instead of focusing on their weaknesses. By looking for the good in your culture, you can create a more engaged workforce.

Here are ideas you can use from other manufacturers:

A GM placed a notebook by the time clock. After employees punched in, they were invited to share a happy thought, a quote, or something they were grateful for before starting their shift. It took a little while to catch on, but the manager shares he has seen a difference in employee attitudes since implementing this simple strategy.

A shop has a "Gratitude Wall" in their lunch room. Employees can write positive notes, happy news or they can simply draw a smiley face on the white board if that's what they want to do. It's colorful and fun. When the board gets filled up, the manager takes a picture, wipes the board down and starts over.

Action ideas:

1. Post positive quotes or pictures by coffee machine or other high traffic areas.

2. Encourage and endorse random acts of kindness throughout the day.

3. Smile and say "hi" to twice as many people as you normally do.

Hire a photographer to take professional headshots.

Show your employees in their best light by taking individual and departmental photographs. Great photos elicit an emotional response, and people want to feel good about themselves. Give them the opportunity to do so.

By providing pictures for your employees' use, you help them look more polished in their social media and other profiles, thereby representing your company more professionally. Grainy images cut from vacation photographs do not look very professional.

Incorporating your staff's current, relevant photos into personalized greeting cards are a terrific way to connect with your customers. Take fun group shots and include them on thank you notes and holiday cards. Have each member of the team sign the card.

Use these photos to put together an org chart with everyone's picture on it. You will give new employees the opportunity to learn who's who in the organization – not only by their title but by their face.

Creative ways to use company photos include:

_____

_____

_____

_____

_____

Take pictures and put them on display.

These days, practically everyone has a high-quality camera that they carry around with them at all times – their phone. Use that tool to have a little fun in the workplace.

Take pictures of your team and hang them on a wall or keep them around the office. Capture a variety of moments – department pictures, event photos, random shots, even what my siblings like to call "stupid family photos." Have fun with it.

Why not have company photo contests and see how many fun, impromptu, action shots you can collect. Have a caption contest for some of the hilarious pictures – and keep it family-friendly, of course.

Sharing photos might not seem like a big deal, but it's a gesture that helps your employees feel like they are part of the team.

Where can you share?

1. Social media – let potential employees know what a great place your company is to work.

2. Bulletin boards – change them up every so often, so people look to see what's new.

3. Slideshow on TVs in the lobby or break room. Show the slideshow during company events. It's always good for a smile.

Let the music play!

Allow your employees to listen to music at work. Researchers from Cornell University discovered that when employees listen to happy, upbeat music, they tend to be more productive, cooperative, and they work harder.

Music is particularly useful when a given task is defined and repetitive. A series of experiments have shown the effectiveness of playing background music while doing repetitive work. Listening to music results in workers performing their tasks more efficiently. These results indicate that there may be an economic benefit to the company when they play music during the workday.

Really, why would you NOT allow your employees to get a little "musical motivation" during the day?

Action Ideas:

1. Let your employees wear ear buds while performing work they can do by themselves.

2. Make sure that safety concerns are taken care of: for example, you might require that employees conceal any wires from ear buds under their clothing, so the wires don't get caught on anything.

3. For a company's intercom system, let team members be the "DJ for the day" and share their personal taste in music (Family friendly, of course)

Keep up-to-date with an intra-company newsletter.

Make your newsletter a fun source of information in the company. Interview employees from different parts of the business. Include fun facts and personal information (as much as they are willing to share).

As your employees discover they have common interests, you'll further encourage friendships to develop. As employees start to "cross the aisle" and get to know team members in other departments, you'll also improve communication levels.

In sharing success stories, make sure you include the accomplishments of your everyone – including your hourly workers. You'll not only give the featured employees the recognition and positive reinforcement they deserve, but you'll also provide a model for other staff to follow.

Ideas for Newsletter features:

1. Success stories or customer spotlights
2. Industry news
3. Human interest stories
4. Educational articles
5. Blog excerpts
6. Coupons or special offers
7. Company Q&A
8. Employee surveys and results
9. Interviews
10. Product reviews
11. Let your imagination run wild!

About the Author

Lisa Ryan is the Chief Appreciation Strategist at Grategy. She helps organizations keep their top talent and best customers from becoming someone else's through her engaging, interactive, and fun keynotes, workshops, and consulting assignments.

Grategy® programs focus on employee productivity and retention, customer loyalty, and overall growth. She is the author of nine books and co-stars in two films, including the award-winning "The Keeper of the Keys" and "The Gratitude Experiment."

In addition to Grategy®, Lisa Ryan is a Regional Director with Leadership USA Cleveland. Leadership USA is a membership organization that offers high-quality leadership education for leaders of our member companies, via a monthly learning event with world-class instructors, who present on diverse topics.

Bring Lisa to your next event:

www.LisaRyanSpeaks,

lisa@grategy.com

216-359-1134.

Bibliography

49 Employee Engagement Ideas (The Ultimate Cheat Sheet Your Team Will Love), Tim Eisenhauer, https://axerosolutions.com/blogs/timeisenhauer/pulse/206/49-employee-engagement-ideas-the-ultimate-cheat-sheet-your-team-will-love

Careers, Jobs, Employees, HR Practitioners, Benefits, Leave, SES, Training, Human Capital U.S. Department of Commerce, Office of the Secretary, Office of Human Resources Management - http://hr.commerce.gov/AboutOHRM/PROD01_009669

Five Lessons Only Failure Can Teach You. Liz Ryan. https://www.forbes.com/sites/lizryan/2015/12/29/five-lessons-only-failure-can-teach-you/2/#6c8162cc39d5

How to Have an Effective Morning 'Ops' Meeting http://www.forconstructionpros.com/construction-technology/personnel-management/article/10302249/how-to-have-an-effective-morning-ops-meeting

How to Increase the Motivation of Factory Workers. Andreas Slotosch. https://beekeeper.io/how-to-increase-the-motivation-of-factory-workers/

How to Select the Employee of the Month. Paula Clapon.
http://www.gethppy.com/employeerecognition/select-employee-of-the-month

Please Micromanage Me, Said No Employee Ever. Lauren Lee
Anderson. https://www.15five.com/blog/please-micromanage-me-said-no-employee-ever/

Talent Management in Manufacturing: The Need for a Fresh
Approach. PWC.com white paper.
https://www.pwc.com/gx/en/industrial-manufacturing/publications/assets/pwc-talent-management.pdf

The Advantages of Promotion from Within, Beth Greenwood.
http://work.chron.com/advantages-promotion-within-6320.html

The Power of Positivity, In Moderation: The Losada Ratio
http://happierhuman.com/losada-ratio/

The Triple Bottom Line: Measuring Your Organization's Wider
Impact.
https://www.mindtools.com/pages/article/newSTR_79.htm

These 6 Companies Give Their Employees Unlimited Tuition Reimbursement. Claire Zillman. http://fortune.com/2016/03/04/companies-employees-tuition-reimbursement/

Top Complaints from Employees About Their Leaders. Lou Solomon. https://hbr.org/2015/06/the-top-complaints-from-employees-about-their-leaders

Why 2016 is the Year for Veterans in the Workplace. Justin Constantine. http://www.industryweek.com/workforce/why-2016-year-veterans-workplace

Why Promoting from Within Usually Beats Hiring from Outside. Susan Adams. http://www.forbes.com/sites/susanadams/2012/04/05/why-promoting-from-within-usually-beats-hiring-from-outside/#75331bea3fb2

Why Should Companies and Employees Have Shared Values. Scott MacFarland, http://www.huffingtonpost.com/scott-macfarland/why-should-companies-and-_b_4225199.html

Order *Manufacturing Engagement* for your next conference, workshop, retreat, or training program where you need ideas and strategies to jumpstart your engagement initiative.

Quantity pricing for direct purchase of the book. All discounts are savings from the retail price of $19.95.

25-100	$15.00 each
101-250	$14.00 each
250-499	$12.00 each
500 +	$10.00 each

Prices do not include shipping and handling.

Call for a complete pricing proposal or an estimate to your location.

Call or email: (216) 359-1134 or lisa@grategy.com

Visit our website for all the latest news:

www.LisaRyanSpeaks.com